MW01234447

The KidHaven Science Library

Magnets

by Kris Hirschmann

KIDHAVEN PRESS
An imprint of Thomson Gale, a part of The Thomson Corporation

THOMSON

GALE

Detroit • New York • San Francisco • San Diego • New Haven, Conn. • Waterville, Maine • London • Munich

For more information, contact
KidHaven Press
27500 Drake Rd.
Farmington Hills, MI 48331-3535
Or you can visit our Internet site at http://www.gale.com

LIBRARY OF CONGRESS CATALOGING-IN-PUBLICATION DATA

Hirschmann, Kris, 1967-
   Magnets / by Kris Hirschmann.
      p. cm. — (The Kidhaven science library)
   Summary: Explains what magnets are, how they changed the world, how they are used in everyday life, and high-tech applications for magnets.
   Includes bibliographical references and index.
   ISBN 0-7377-1016-0 (hbk. : alk. paper)
   1. Magnets—Juvenile literature. 2. Magnetic applications –Juvenile literature. [1. Magnets. 2. Magnetic power.] I. Title.
   II. Series.

Contents

Chapter 1

What Are Magnets?

Magnets are one of the Earth's natural wonders. These objects can attract certain metals. They can stick to some materials, and they can push other magnets away without touching them. Because the forces that make these things happen are invisible, people once thought magnets were magical. But today, scientists know that there is nothing mysterious or supernatural about magnets. These objects get their power from everyday materials and properties that just happen to have some remarkable effects.

Magnet Materials

Some magnets are found in nature. Natural magnets are sometimes called **lodestones**. Lodestones are rocks made mostly of the minerals iron and oxygen, which join to form a material called magnetite. Magnetite is found all over the world, but deposits are especially common in parts of Europe, Russia, Peru, and the United States.

Magnets can also be created artificially in labs or factories. Artificial magnets are often shaped like bars, disks, or horseshoes. They may be made from many different materials. Alnico magnets, for example, are a mixture of iron, aluminum, nickel, and cobalt. Ferrite magnets are a mixture of an iron **oxide** (an iron-oxygen **compound**) with other oxides. And rare-earth magnets combine iron with hard-to-find minerals such as neodymium and samarium. Rare-earth magnets are the strongest type. But they are expensive, so they are used mostly when people need small but powerful magnets. For everyday needs, ferrite magnets are by far the most common.

Magnets come in many different shapes and sizes.

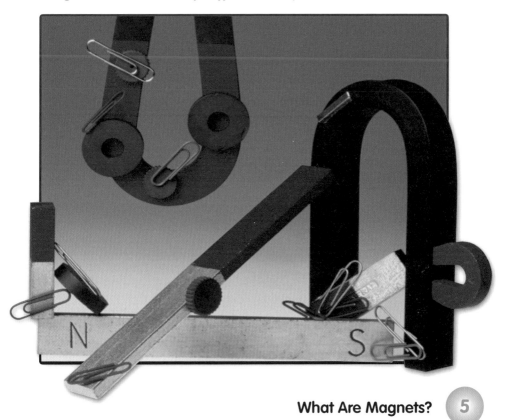

Whether they are natural or artificial, all magnets pull on certain metals. Metals that feel this pull are called **magnetic**. Only four metals—iron, steel, cobalt, and nickel—are strongly magnetic. All other materials are considered nonmagnetic. This means they are not attracted to magnets, or they are attracted so weakly that the pull is not noticeable. A magnetic force can pass right through these materials and attract metal objects on the other side.

How Magnets Work

Magnets get their amazing properties from their **atoms**—the tiny building blocks that combine to build all matter. Each atom contains particles, some of which carry electrical charges. In magnetic materials, the atoms have properties that make them join into tiny regions called **domains**. Within a domain, all of the atoms point in the same direction. The electrical charges of their particles work together to create a very weak magnetic pull.

A single object may contain a huge number of domains. In most materials, these domains are all jumbled together in no particular order. They pull in many different directions, so they cancel each other out. In a magnet, however, the domains line up so they all point the same way. This means they are pulling together. When thousands

How to Make Your Own Magnet

> **Materials:** 1 magnet
> 1 needle
> several paper clips

1. Hold the magnet between your fingers and rub the needle across it in one direction. Lift the needle at the end of each pass. Rub it across the magnet at least fifty times. Take care not to prick yourself with the sharp end of the needle.

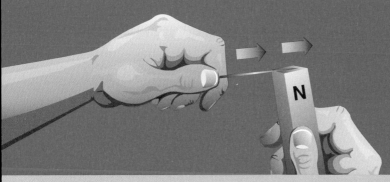

2. Hold the needle close to some paper clips and see if it picks them up. Repeat step 1 if the needle is not yet magnetized.

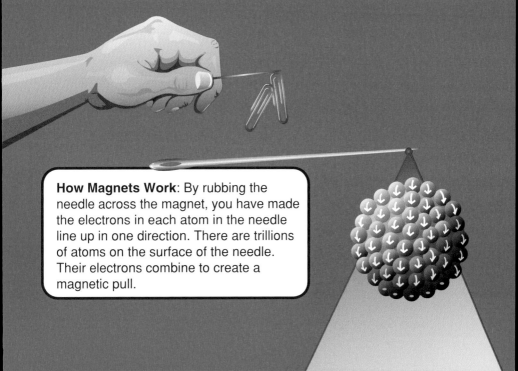

How Magnets Work: By rubbing the needle across the magnet, you have made the electrons in each atom in the needle line up in one direction. There are trillions of atoms on the surface of the needle. Their electrons combine to create a magnetic pull.

of domains pull in the same direction, they create a magnetic force that is strong enough to affect other materials.

Two Poles

All magnets have two **poles**, or sides where the magnetic force is strongest. These sides are called the north pole and the south pole. When two magnets are held close together, their opposite

A horseshoe magnet attracts clusters of iron filings.

poles (north and south) attract each other. Their similar poles (north and north or south and south) push each other away. Both poles attract magnetic materials that are not magnets themselves.

The area around a magnet that can attract things is called the **magnetic field**. The magnetic field is invisible. It consists of countless lines of force that arc from one of the magnet's poles to the other. The field is strongest near the magnet's poles. So in these regions, the lines are very close together. Farther from the poles, the field is weaker, and the lines are more spread out. It is possible to see the shape and spacing of these lines by shaking some metal filings

Iron filings, transformed into tiny magnets, form patterns around a bar magnet.

onto a piece of paper. When a magnet is held beneath the paper, the filings arrange themselves in the shape of the magnetic field.

The size and strength of a magnetic field depend on the size and strength of the magnet. Tiny chips of magnetite, for example, have tiny magnetic fields.

Larger magnets have bigger and stronger fields. The largest magnetic field on Earth belongs to the Earth itself. The Earth acts as an enormous magnet because its core is filled with molten iron. When the Earth spins, the iron slowly churns. This motion creates a massive magnetic field that stretches more than 37,000 miles (59,546km) into space. The poles of this field lie near (but not exactly at) the planet's geographic North and South poles.

Permanent Versus Temporary

There are two main types of magnets. Magnets that work all the time (for example, refrigerator magnets) are called hard magnets or permanent magnets. The natural structure of hard magnets keeps the domains fixed in one position. Because the domains are always lined up, these materials always exert a magnetic pull.

Other magnets work only when needed. These are called soft magnets or temporary magnets. In a soft magnet, the domains are usually mixed up. When an outside force is applied, however, the domains line up and turn the material into a magnet. As soon as the force is removed, the domains get mixed up again, and the magnet loses its power.

A paper clip can be used to show how a soft magnet works. Paper clips do not usually attract metal objects. But when a paper clip touches a hard magnet, its domains line up. The paper clip is now a

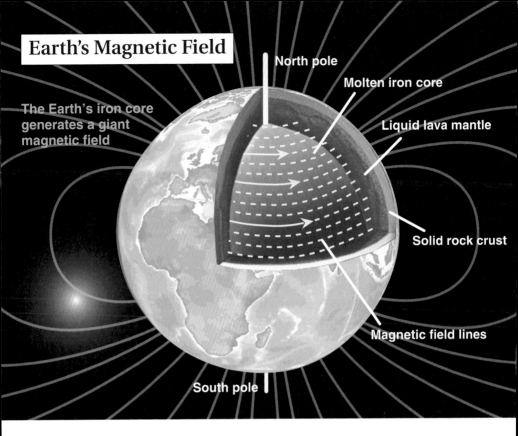

Earth's Magnetic Field

The Earth's iron core generates a giant magnetic field

North pole

Molten iron core

Liquid lava mantle

Solid rock crust

Magnetic field lines

South pole

magnet itself and can even attract other paper clips. It keeps its power until it loses contact with the hard magnet.

In technology and industry, soft magnets have many advantages. They can be much larger than hard magnets. It is possible to adjust their strength as needed, and they can even be turned off when they are not in use. These properties make soft magnets very useful in some situations. But when constant pulling power is needed—to hold a note to the refrigerator, for instance—nothing but a hard magnet will do. Both temporary and permanent magnets have their uses, and both are just as important in today's world.

Chapter 2

Magnets Changed the World

People have known about natural magnets for many thousands of years. In the earliest days, magnets were just a curiosity. But over the centuries, humans came up with many uses for these helpful objects. Some of these uses were so important that they changed the world forever. It is fair to say that without magnets, society and technology as we know them today would not exist.

The Early History of Magnets

Lodestones were described in the earliest Greek writings. From these texts, it is clear that people had seen lodestones and their **magnetism** at work. They did not, however, know quite what to make of these odd rocks. Scholars of the time thought lodestones were strange and mysterious. They were marvels without a purpose.

The first use for lodestones seems to have developed in China. Sometime around 200 B.C., the Chinese discovered that these rocks would align themselves in a north-south direction if they were allowed to swivel freely. Today, scientists know that magnets line up with the Earth's magnetic field. This is what caused the effect the Chinese observed. At the time, however, no one knew about magnetic fields, so the lodestone's behavior was puzzling— but interesting nonetheless. Chinese artisans began carving large lodestones into the shape of long-handled spoons. When a magnetic spoon was set on a smooth bronze plate, it rotated until its handle pointed south.

Lodestone, also called magnetite, exerts a weak magnetic pull.

The magnetic needle of a compass always points north, and allows users to determine their direction of travel.

It was to be 800 years before the next leap in knowledge was made. But when the leap came, it was a big one. Around A.D. 600, Chinese crafts-people figured out how to turn small bits of iron into magnets. When these magnets floated on water, they aligned themselves in a north-south direction, just as the spoons had. This discovery paved the way for one of humankind's most important inventions: the **compass**.

The Compass

A compass is a device that contains a magnetic needle. This needle always lines up with the Earth's magnetic fields. It is mounted in a way that lets it spin freely. So no matter how the compass is held, the needle always turns until it points north and south. By looking at the needle, a person can figure out not only north and south but also east, west, and all other directions in between.

The compass was a very useful tool for **navigation**. It was small and easy to carry. Its needle also moved instantly as the compass's position changed. These features made it practical to keep compasses on ships—and this change had a huge impact on sea travel. Before compasses were invented, sailors had to find their way by looking at the stars. This method worked fine when conditions were good. A few days of bad weather, though, could throw a ship far off course. The compass changed all that. With these devices on board, sailors could figure out where they were even if they could not see the sky.

A compass is used to navigate a sailboat on its journey.

By making sea travel less risky, compasses affected the way people lived. In the Mediterranean and much of Europe, for example, traders felt safe enough to sail during bad-weather times of the year as well as good-weather times. Compasses also gave Christopher Columbus and other famous explorers the courage to strike out for unknown lands. These brave men knew that no matter how far they sailed, they would always be able to find their way back home.

Compasses were essential in travel until a few decades ago. Today, devices that use satellite information have mostly replaced compasses on ships and airplanes. But compasses are still important for hikers and other people who enjoy the wilderness, and they are used as backups in all major forms of travel.

Electricity Makes Magnets

The next key discovery about magnets was made hundreds of years after the compass was invented. In 1819 a Danish scientist named Hans Christian Oersted noticed that a compass needle moved if it was placed near an electric current. He realized that electricity and magnetism must be related somehow. This principle became known as electromagnetism.

Scientists everywhere were excited by Oersted's discovery. They started to run experiments, and soon a new discovery was made. In 1825 a British inventor named William Sturgeon coiled wire around an iron core. When he sent electricity through the coil, he was astonished to find that the iron became a magnet. When the electricity was turned off, the iron went back to its normal state. Sturgeon had invented the world's first **electromagnet**—a magnet that can be turned on and off like a lightbulb.

A wire connects the copper coils of a simple electromagnet, creating a magnetic field that lifts iron filings.

Electromagnets proved to be incredibly useful. The fact that they could be switched off made them much easier to handle and store than regular magnets. By using bigger cores and more coils, people could also create exceptionally large and strong electromagnets. These objects were soon being used in all types of technology, from telephones to telegraphs and much more. This trend has continued all the way to the present. Today, electromagnets are built into thousands of devices that people use every day.

Electricity does not just make temporary magnets. It makes permanent ones as well. In the early 1900s, scientists discovered that certain materials became magnets for good if they were exposed to a strong electrical current. Soon, factories all over the world were churning out magnets in many shapes and sizes. Just like electromagnets, permanent magnets quickly found their way into all sorts of devices.

Magnets Make Electricity

Another important discovery about magnets came in 1831. In this year, a British scientist named Michael Faraday discovered that the relationship between magnetism and electricity works both ways. In other words, not only does electricity make magnets; magnets can also make electricity. Using magnets to create electricity is called **induction**.

Michael Faraday, pictured with magnet in hand, discovered new information about magnetism and electricity.

Induction is very simple in principle. A changing magnetic field makes a current flow through copper, aluminum, or any other material that conducts electricity. The changing field can come either from a magnet moving near a still piece of metal or from metal moving near a still magnet. Either way, the

A magnet powered this early electric motor, invented in England in 1839. The design built on Michael Faraday's work.

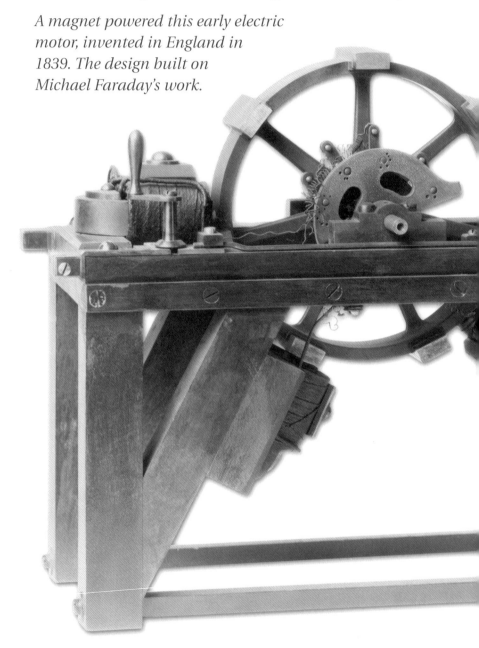

current continues as long as the motion does. The instant the motion stops, the current stops flowing as well.

Soon after Faraday discovered the principle of induction, he figured out how to put it to work. He built a small device that spun a copper disk between the poles of a horseshoe magnet. This motion created a weak electric current. Faraday had succeeded in building the world's first electromagnetic **generator**.

Faraday's little generator was simple, but its consequences were not. By proving that magnets could create usable electricity, this device opened up a whole new area of scientific exploration. As researchers started inventing new ways to use Faraday's discovery, induction became more and more important in modern technologies. Today, induction is used in the world's biggest generators to make electricity for cities. It is also at work in many household devices. Many things that define today's world could not exist without the power of magnets.

Chapter 3

Magnets in Everyday Life

If someone asked a hundred people to name a use for magnets, "sticking things to the fridge" would probably be the most common response. Refrigerator magnets are certainly very helpful. Decorative magnets can secure notes and artwork, for example, and printed magnetic sheets keep useful information like pizza delivery numbers and the local vet's address in plain view. These very visible magnets, however, are far from the only magnets people use regularly. Everyday life is filled with these useful objects.

Magnets Around the House

Permanent magnets are scattered all over most people's homes. One common use is to keep doors closed. Refrigerator doors, for example, are lined with strips of magnetized rubber. This rubber sticks to the refrigerator's metal frame and holds the door shut without the need for latches.

Fanciful magnets adorn refrigerators in many American households today.

A fish appears to float in midair in this new Japanese toy. The effect is created by a hidden magnet and electric coil.

Magnets may also keep kitchen cupboards, bathroom cabinets, and other doors shut tight.

Magnets are also used around the house for grabbing metal objects. Most electric can openers, for instance, have round magnets that keep metal lids from falling onto the kitchen counter. Magnetized screwdrivers make it much easier to control screws before they are driven into walls or wood. So do magnetic bowls, which are very handy in home workshops. Even if these bowls tip upside down, the metal objects inside will not tumble out.

Magnetic Toys

Many toys contain magnets. Children learn to read, for example, with the help of magnetic letters and numbers that can be arranged on a metal surface. They may draw with magnet-tipped pens on plastic pads filled with metal shavings. The shavings leap upward when the pen passes over, creating dark lines. Magnetic fishing games and travel games are popular, as are magnetic dress-up dolls. Magnetic construction kits are fun and better than traditional blocks in some ways, since the pieces stick together. And for the grown-up crowd, there are desk toys that come with magnetic bases and dozens of small steel shapes. When the shapes are placed on the base, they become temporary magnets. The metal pile can be stacked and stuck together in countless ways to form a different sculpture every day.

Magnets in Home Technology

Home entertainment is another magnet-filled area. Videotapes and sound cassettes, for example, contain plastic tape that is covered with magnetic particles. On a blank tape, the particles are all lined up. On a recorded tape, the particles point in many different directions. The pattern of the particles determines the information on the tape.

To read recorded information, VCRs and cassette players wind the tape past magnets. Due to induction, this motion causes a changing electric current. The player sends the current to a TV, speakers, or both, where devices translate it into forms people can understand. Magnets inside the TV, for example, help change the current into the images that appear on the screen. At the same time, magnets inside the speakers change the current into vibrations. These vibrations travel through the air and into people's ears, where they are heard as sound.

Magnets are also an important part of every computer. Like VCRs and cassette players, computers use magnets to record and read information on floppy disks and hard drives. Their monitors use magnets to produce images, and their speakers contain magnets that change electricity into sound.

People who want to keep their computers and TVs safe sometimes use another magnet-driven technology in homes and businesses: the security alarm system. In these systems, small but powerful magnets are attached to each window and door. When the doors and windows are shut, the magnets attract bits of metal in devices mounted nearby. This pull acts like a switch to keep the system turned off. If the doors or windows are opened unexpectedly, the pull is lost, and the alarm turns on with a loud and frightening blare.

Magnets Out and About

There are just as many magnets outside the home as within. These objects are especially common on roadways, where they are found in cars, trucks, buses, and motorcycles. Buried deep inside electric

Electric motors with magnets power windshield wipers, windows, and other common features of cars and trucks.

motors, small magnets help open and close windows, raise and lower radio antennas, move windshield wipers back and forth, and much more. As at home, they also create the music that flows out of a vehicle's speakers.

An electromagnetic crane lifts and moves tons of scrap metal at a Japanese recycling center.

Banks and stores are another good place to find magnets. These objects are used anytime someone gets money or pays for goods with a credit or debit card. Credit and debit cards have magnetic strips that hold recorded information, much like the plastic tape inside music and video cassettes. The strips are swiped past magnets when they need to be read.

More Uses for Magnets

A quick drive to the local dump shows a much larger magnet at work. Here, giant electromagnets are used to move old cars and other metal junk. The magnet dangles from a crane above anything that needs to be picked up. When the magnet is switched on, it clings tightly to the metal garbage. The crane moves the object to another part of the dump. The electromagnet is then turned off, and the object falls to its new resting place.

A less visible but equally common use of magnets occurs on farms. Here, farmers feed magnets shaped like giant pills to young cattle. These magnets, which are appropriately known as "cow magnets," stay in a cow's stomach forever. Any stray bits of metal the cow eats by accident will stick to the magnet. This stops the metal from traveling through the cow's system and hurting or even killing the animal.

Magnets and Health

Some people think magnets have an effect on human health. They say that living in the Earth's magnetic field makes humans sensitive to magnetism of all types. They also point out that human blood contains iron, which is attracted to magnets. So if a magnet is placed on the skin, the theory goes, it should pull on the blood below. This process should have measurable effects on a person's physical state.

Some health professionals believe that magnetic bracelets and necklaces can help patients with conditions like arthritis.

A large area of alternative medicine is based on this belief. People can buy magnetic bracelets to treat hand and wrist pain, anklets to treat foot and ankle pain, and necklaces to treat headaches. Pains in other areas can be treated with stick-on magnet patches or large magnetic wraps. Magnetic wristbands are a common treatment for seasickness, while other magnets are said to cure certain diseases. And for all-over good health, magnetic mattresses and pillows are even available. The people who sell these items say that they lower the body's stress level, which makes it possible to get a better night's sleep.

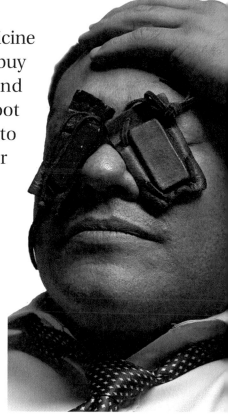

Seeking relief from sinus pain, a man undergoes treatment with magnets at a Mexico City clinic.

It would be wonderful if magnets did everything their supporters claimed. There is, however, no hard evidence that magnets actually improve health. But the lack of evidence does not make a difference to true believers. Many people swear that magnets make them feel better. Whether this effect is real or all in the mind, there is no doubt that it is good for those who experience it. It is one more way that magnets make the world a better place for people everywhere.

Chapter 4

High-Tech Magnets

Magnets are not just useful in everyday life. They are also important tools for scientists and researchers around the world. Some of today's most original and cutting-edge technologies are made possible by magnets.

Superconducting Magnets

The most powerful magnets today are called superconducting magnets. In these high-tech electromagnets, the wire coil that surrounds the core is cooled to a very low temperature. Cooling the wire lets electricity flow very easily. This means more power can move through the wire, which in turn increases the power of the electromagnet. The strongest superconducting magnets can produce fields nearly 800,000 times greater than the one generated by Earth.

Superconducting magnets are a big help to scientists everywhere. They are especially useful in the study of atoms. These particles are much too small to be examined individually. But when many atoms are controlled by magnets, some of their properties can be measured.

To study atoms, scientists sometimes use enormous circular tubes called particle accelerators. The tubes are surrounded by hundreds or even thousands of superconducting magnets. When the magnets are switched on, their enormously powerful fields push the atoms inside the tube.

Scientists in Switzerland use these superconducting magnets to help them learn more about atoms and matter.

The atoms zip around and around until they reach incredibly high speeds. Scientists then smash the atoms together and watch how they react. Over the past few decades, particle accelerators have taught researchers many new things about matter and energy.

Medical Magnets

Superconducting magnets are not just found in labs. Today, they play an important role in hospitals and other medical centers as well. They are most com-

Superconducting magnets like those used inside this medical scanner help doctors see inside a person's body.

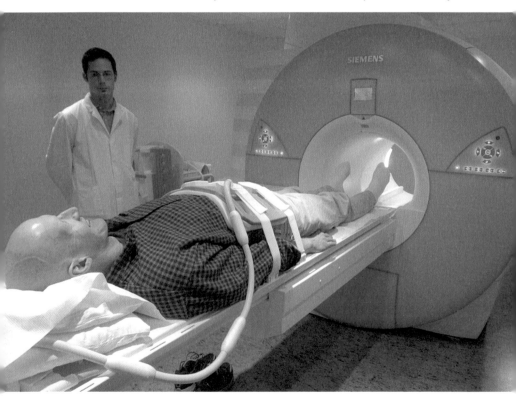

mon in machines that do magnetic resonance imaging, better known as MRI.

MRI devices are like large boxes with tubes in the middle. A person lies in the tube. Hidden by the machine's plastic walls are several doughnut-shaped superconducting magnets that surround the patient. When these magnets are switched on, they create a magnetic field about 20,000 times stronger than normal. The patient feels nothing—but the atoms of his or her body do. They react in tiny ways to the magnetic field. A computer measures the reactions and turns them into pictures.

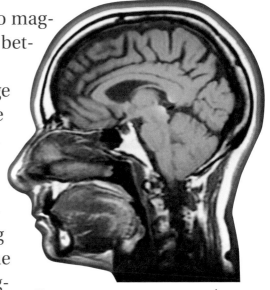

Doctors can scan a person's brain and other body parts using magnetic resonance imaging (MRI) to detect tumors or other abnormalities.

Looking at MRI pictures, doctors can spot tumors and other problems inside a person's body without using surgery or drugs. Not only is this process easier on patients, it also lets doctors see very tiny problems that they might miss during surgery. By improving the diagnostic process, MRI has revolutionized the world of medicine.

MRI devices are not the only magnetic tools used in the field of medicine. In hospitals and doctors' offices, magnets come in handy for all sorts of things. Magnet-bearing probes, for example, can safely remove pins and other metal objects from patients' stomachs. Other types of magnets can suck metal shards out of people's eyes and skin. For reasons not clearly understood by scientists: electromagnets sometimes speed the healing time of bone fractures. And regular magnets can hold needles, dentures, and other objects in place. Using magnets in these ways and others can make medical procedures safer, easier, and more effective.

Floating Trains

Some day in the near future, people may travel to their medical appointments on magnetically powered trains. These high-speed, floating vehicles are

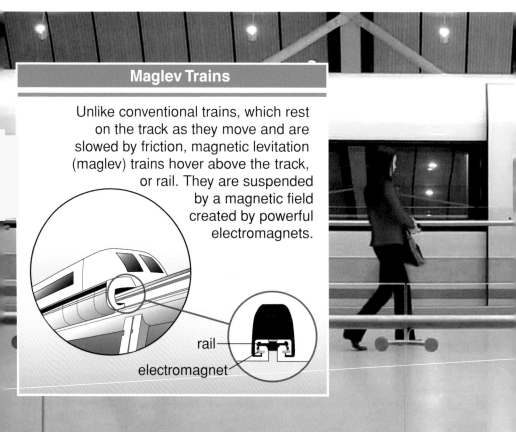

Maglev Trains

Unlike conventional trains, which rest on the track as they move and are slowed by friction, magnetic levitation (maglev) trains hover above the track, or rail. They are suspended by a magnetic field created by powerful electromagnets.

rail

electromagnet

being tested around the world today. The technology that drives them is called magnetic levitation, or **maglev** for short. Superconducting magnets are built into maglev trains and their tracks. The magnets are arranged with their opposite poles facing each other. Some of the magnets push each other apart hard enough to make a train float a little bit, separating its moving parts from the tracks. Others push at each other sideways, creating a force that shoves the train forward or backward.

Maglev trains are better in some ways than regular trains. They do not touch their tracks, so they are a lot quieter. They can also travel much faster.

A high-speed maglev train prepares to depart from a station in Shanghai, China.

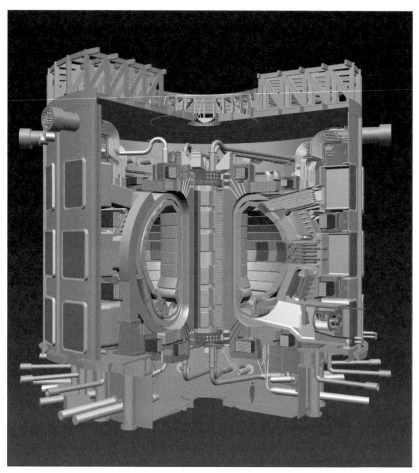

Sophisticated magnets are part of an experimental device (pictured in this computer model) that may one day provide a new source of energy.

One passenger-carrying line in China, for example, has a top speed of 268 miles per hour (431km), and an experimental Japanese train has reached 363 miles per hour (584km). But despite these advantages, only a few maglev systems exist today. Maglev technology is fairly new, so maglev trains are more expensive than regular trains. The new technology is also harder to fix if it breaks down. As maglev technology gets better and cheaper, communities may become more willing to build these magnetic marvels.

Maglev technology may have another use as well. Some space agencies, including the National Aeronautics and Space Administration (NASA), are trying to figure out how to use magnets to launch spacecraft. Scientists estimate that a magnet-powered rocket could be 30 percent lighter than one without magnets. Lighter spacecraft would need less fuel, so launching them would be much less expensive than it is today.

Magnetic Art

When scientists conduct cutting-edge research, they are usually looking for practical ways to use new technology. But a company called TechnoFrolics is more interested in high-tech fun. This company has developed a computer-controlled tray with electromagnets in its base. The top part of the

Iron dust fills the top part of a TechnoFrolics tray.

tray is filled with iron dust. By changing the flow of electricity to the electromagnets, computer programs magnetize the dust in different ways from one moment to the next. This process makes the dust dance and swirl above the tray, with iron peaks swaying back and forth like underwater sea grass. The dust keeps time with music, and it does things that reflect the music's mood.

David Durlach, the founder of TechnoFrolics, originally thought of his dancing dust trays as an art form. He saw no need for them to be useful or practical. But other people enjoy Durlach's creations so much that they are finding ways to put them to work. Several dancing dust exhibits are now being shown at museums across the United States. TechnoFrolics also created an iron-dust "living logo" for the Ford Motor Company. The dust in this display takes the shape of Ford's logo while it dances to music.

Odds and Ends

Durlach's inventions are unique in their field. But in the big picture, they are just one of many interesting discoveries in the study of magnetics. Companies everywhere are finding new uses for high-tech magnets. In the steel industry, for example, powerful electromagnets can hold heavy steel objects while they are being shaped. This use makes clamps unnecessary. In the home-improvement industry, magnets

Sophisticated magnets such as this one at a Swiss laboratory may help scientists unlock the secrets of life.

may be used to remove minerals from drinking water. In the space industry, liquids are sometimes magnetized so they can be controlled by magnets in gravity-free conditions. In medicine, researchers are inventing ways to kill cancer cells with tiny magnets. And in labs, scientists use maglev techniques to handle dangerous materials.

The sheer number of uses for magnets is staggering. Even more amazing, though, is the thought of the countless discoveries yet to come. People have not even come close to figuring out everything magnets can do. As the years go by, scientists are sure to find more and better ways to put magnets and their incredible forces to work.

Glossary

atoms: The tiny building blocks that combine to build all matter.

compass: A device with a magnetic needle that always points north.

compound: A substance that is made from two or more other substances.

domains: Regions whose atoms all point in the same direction. Every domain has a magnetic pull.

electromagnet: A temporary magnet that has a metal core surrounded by coils of wire. The core becomes a magnet when electricity flows through the wire.

generator: A machine that turns motion into electricity.

induction: Using magnets to create electricity.

lodestones: A name for natural magnets.

maglev: Short for magnetic levitation, which is the use of magnets to lift things off the ground.

magnetic: Able to feel a magnet's pull.

magnetic field: The area around a magnet that can affect magnetic materials.

magnetism: The attracting property that magnets possess.

navigation: In travel, the science of figuring out distances, locations, and directions.

oxide: A compound of oxygen and one or more other elements.

poles: The parts of a magnet where the magnetic field is strongest.

Books

Paul Doherty and John Cassidy, *Magnetic Magic: Magic Tricks Done with Magnets*. Palo Alto, CA: Klutz, 1994. This book is full of magnetic ways to astonish people! Make magnets float, turn regular butter knives into magnets, make paper clips and coins appear out of thin air, and much more.

Calvin Hall and Daryl Pederson, *Northern Lights: The Science, Myth, and Wonder of Aurora Borealis*. Seattle, WA: Sasquatch, 2001. Northern lights occur when particles interact with the Earth's magnetic field. This book is full of amazing pictures of this phenomenon.

Marylou Morano Kjelle, *Raymond Damadian and the Development of MRI*. Bear, DE: Mitchell Lane, 2003. Read about the man who invented MRI technology in this interesting biography.

Shar Levine and Leslie Johnstone, *The Magnet Book*. New York: Sterling, 1997. This excellent book introduces basic information about magnets, and details science experiments based on each concept.

Sharon Sharth, *Way to Go! Finding Your Way with a Compass*. Pleasantville, NY: Reader's Digest, 2000. Learn everything you need to know about finding direction with a compass.

Web Sites

MagLev: Moving into the Future (www.ic.sunysb.edu/Stu/ppoggio/maglev/index.html). This kid-friendly site is helpful in understanding maglev technology. It also helps users think about the best ways and places to use maglev systems.

Magnet Man (www.coolmagnetman.com). This site features lots of basic magnet information, plus easy science experiments anyone can do with magnets.

TechnoFrolics (www.technofrolics.net). See dancing iron dust in action along with some other magnetic marvels.

Index

Picture Credits

About the Author

Kris Hirschmann has written more than 100 books for children. She owns and runs The Wordshop (www.the-wordshop.com), a business that provides a variety of writing and editorial services. She holds a bachelor's degree in psychology from Dartmouth College in Hanover, New Hampshire.

Hirschmann lives just outside Orlando, Florida, with her husband, Michael, and her daughters, Nikki and Erika.